The Life and Works of

Marie Laveau

Gris-Gris • Cleansings
Charms • Hexes

by Raul Canizares

ORIGINAL PUBLICATIONS
PLAINVIEW, NEW YORK

THE LIFE AND WORKS OF MARIE LAVEAU
By Raul Canizares

© ORIGINAL PUBLICATIONS 2001

ISBN: 0-942272-71-4

FIRST EDITION
First Printing 2001

Cover art and interior illustrations by Raul Canizares

Original Publications
P.O. Box 236
Old Bethpage, New York 11804-0236
(516) 454-6809

Printed in the United States of America

DEDICATION:
For Narayan Ramos and John Andolina

INTRODUCTION

Ever since I was a little boy in Cuba, relatives who visited from New Orleans sparked a great interest in me about "The Big Easy." So great was my fascination with New Orleans that my Madrina, Priestess of Obatala Amanda Gomez, concluded that in a past life I had been famed Voodoo king Dr. John. At the age of seventeen, my dream of living in New Orleans came true when an opportunity arose allowing me to move there. A friend of my mother's called La Mora, and her husband Ito, helped us rent a lovely little apartment in Elysian Fields Avenue and Abundance Street, in the early seventies the center of the small Cuban community in New Orleans. Since the first day I walked through the French Quarter, I knew that somehow I had come home again.

The Santería elders under whose tutelage I continued my studies in New Orleans, begun in Cuba ten years before, frowned upon my fascination with New Orleans Voodoo and my desire to study it, thinking that one crowned a Santero shouldn't "lower himself" to studying "lesser forms" of magic. My heart was so set on studying Voodoo, however, that La Mora nudged Ito into taking me to meet his friend, a bona-fide voodoo doctor named Willie Glapion.

La Mora and Ito were a striking couple. Both were Cuban and spoke only Spanish, but at a time when not too many black Cubans had migrated to the U.S., their total blackness set them apart from other Cubans in the area, most of whom were white. La Mora resembled the actress Hattie McDaniels and she dressed like her character *"Mammy"* in the motion picture *"Gone with the Wind."* Ito looked like Bill "Bojangles" Robinson. At 64, La Mora was a priestess of Yemaya, but since she had made Santo only one year previously, I was her elder even though I was only seventeen! Ito had not made Santo, but was a devout believer nonetheless.

"Willie don't accept no students and very few clients, Lil'Baba" Ito told me. "He don't even let me bring La Mora with me when I go see him. But he works as a supervisor of maintenance down at the Times-Picayune where I work, if you're willing to work, I'll get you a job there and you can meet him there yourself, then you can use your Cuban charm to snake your way into his confidence!"

Before I knew what hit me, I was cleaning a composing room so dirty I thought I was going to faint.

"This room gets just as doity every day, boy" the stern-looking old man told me "so you might as well just quit now, there's no way youse gonna make it."

His accent was the weirdest I'd ever heard. It was a mixture of South, Black, French, and Brooklyn!, The Brooklyn part threw me off, until Ito told me that in the old days the overseer of the largest plantation in the area had been from Brooklyn so that large numbers of slaves who learned English from hira spoke with a Brooklyn accent *"Big wheel keep on toining, proud Mary keep on boining."*

In those days before computers, a newspaper's composing room was a nightmare to clean. Every single letter in that paper was set by hand, extremely able specialists literally setting the type little metal letters by hand, one by one, composing the way each page would look, thus the name "composing room". The frenzied activity in this room, where about 100 people worked at a manic pace with metal, paper, wood, and ink, created each night approximately 2500 pounds of garbage and an ink stained nightmare no living man seemed able to clean by himself, except Ol' Man Tacho, a seventy-year-old Honduran alcoholic who had held the job for fifty years. According to Ito, the routine was always the same, Tacho would go on an alcoholic binge and get lost for a few days, he would then be fired only to be rehired when the tightwad bosses at the Picayune realized that it literally took at least ten men to do half the job Tacho did. The result would be that Tacho would inevitably receive a raise. Things got better when Willie Glapion took over as supervisor, for instead of demanding that Tacho be sober, he rationed the old man's intake so he could function while still drinking. It worked, but occasionally, Tacho would be the old Tacho and the same old drama would ensue.

In the meantime, Ito told me to try my best to hang on because in about a week Tacho would come back and I'd be either fired or moved to another--easier--spot, at any rate, although at the time I needed the job, my real purpose for being there, to meet and try to befriend Willie Glapion, would have been accomplished. Sure enough, about a week later Tacho was rehired and Willie offered me another spot Looking at me intensely, Willie told me,

"You know, boy, I's very seldom wrong about things, but I shoh'nuff was wrong about you! I'd seen those smooth, manicured hands and your pale complexion and I said, this white boy ain't lasting one night in dat composing room, yet you not only stuck it out, but you cleaned dat monster almost good as Ol' Man Tacho hisseff."

I thanked Willie for his compliment, and proceeded to tell him I wasn't white, that my great-great-grandfather had been an African slave. Willie let out a huge grin and

WILLIE GLAPION

said,

"You'se an octoroon, just like my mother! She could pass for white; I'd be white-looking too if it weren't cause she fell in love wid a field nigger wid lotsa charm!"

I was nervous because Willie's candor had taken me by surprise. I was intensely aware of race relations in the United States at the time. Martin Luther King's assassination had occurred only four years previously, and the U.S. South was just then beginning to ease its own version of apartheid.

After I had been working at the Picayune for almost three months, Willie said, out of the blue,

"You is a two-headed man, ain't you?"

I was startled and didn't understand his question.

"Come now, don't play dumb. I sees the respec my friend Ito gives you, you a doctor too, right?" Before I had a chance to respond, Willie said, "No need to talk here, you and Ito come to my place dis Sunday and I'll boil us a big pot of swimp and we'll talk."

For the life of me I didn't know what "swimp" were, but I excitedly accepted his invitation. Ito and I usually drove home from work together. I remember nervously asking Ito during our ride back that morning - we worked the 11 PM to 7 AM shift -

"What the hell is `swimp'?" fully expecting to hear either bayou snakes or baby gators.

"Swimp is how the creoles pronounce shrimp, loco, your favorite food, camarones!"

Ito also explained that "twoheaded" was the local way of saying "psychic" or "mediumistic."

"It means you have two heads, one that sees what we all see and the other that sees all that other weird stuff like dead people."

Sundays at Willie's became a routine for Ito and me. Later on the impenetrable Willie became comfortable enough with us to come to our houses, Ito's and mine, and share his inestimable wisdom with my mother and La Mora as well. Willie Glapion, as it turned out, was not only a repository of precious Voodoo recipes and ceremonies, but he was a direct blood descendant and spiritual heir of one of the most fascinating women who ever lived, Marie Laveau, New Orleans' greatest Voodoo queen. For the next two years I was to dedicate the majority of my waking hours and most of my dream time as well to Marie Laveau as interpreted by Willie Glapion. In this book I'll attempt to portray some of what I felt at the time, as well as sharing with the world some of the wisdom of Marie Laveau as well as that of Willie Glapion.

I

To Know Marie Laveau is to Know Voodoo

Ito wasn't sure I should accept initiation into Voodoo. Technically, I didn't need this since I had already been initiated into Haitian Petro Vodou when I was twelve. But in the world of New Orleans Voodoo, each Voodoo priest or priestess who is willing to teach you will initiate you first. I've met people who have had initiation by ten different Voodoo priests. I wanted to learn from Willie Glapion, so I did not hesitate to take initiation from him. It was a simple affair compared to the initiations I'd undergone before. Ito drove me up Elysian Fields all the way to the LSU campus by Lake Pontchartrain, there we were met by an old man in a row boat who took us to the other side of the lake, to a desolate spot totally hidden by Cypress trees at a place called Bayou Tchoupitoulas. We walked about ten minutes before coming upon a large wooden house that seemed to grow out of the ground, as much a part of the scenery as the trees themselves. About five men and two women, all over 50 years of age, were waiting for us. Ito then confessed to me that he had been initiated by Willie years before. While I won't go into the details of the initiation, it involved me taking a ritual bath outside the house, then being blindfolded. I was told to lie naked with arms outstretched in the middle of the temple room. Nine lighted votives were balanced on my body; four on each outstretched arm and one in the middle of my chest. Chicken blood baptized me, cat blood gave me strength, and being hit by the flat side of a machete seven times gave me the ability to fight back. A big snake then slithered over my body, raising a very palpable sort of energy within me as it crossed over my chest. After awhile, the sound and smell of burnt gunpowder told me the ceremony was over. I was now ready to receive instruction from Willie Glapion.

After my initiation, what I thought was Willie's pet snake, but was in reality a holy icon of his faith, became very familiar to me and would come to greet me each time I came to visit. I'd heard that snakes are deaf, but Simbi, as Willie's boa was called, was totally domesticated and came to Willie each time he called her. She lived in a hole in the middle of the temple room. The outside of the hole was always decorated with intricate and beautiful veves, the ideographs that call the spirits down and are more commonly used in Haitian Vodou. For all ceremonies, Willie would call the snake by chanting, in a surprisingly sweet and velvety voice *"L'Appe vini, le Grand Simbi, L'Appe vini, pou fe gris-gris!"* Willie taught us that the reason that snakes represent the divine in Voodoo is because when Mawu-Lisa, the first couple, first came to earth, they were blind, but a snake licked their eyes and then they were able to see. This was in Dahomey, the seat of creation. Since then, the snake has been the Deity's best friend.

About 200 feet from Willie's house, there was a clearing where his little group of *"ageing Voodoos,"* as he called them, would worship Simbi, play drums, dance, and drink tafia, an alcoholic ritual drink that helped us achieve altered

Marie Laveau at age 30
with her pet snake Simbi

states of consciousness. The feast I was privileged to be a part of on St. John's eve was called the *"Danse Calinda,"* a legendary ceremony once popular in New Orleans Voodoo, but in modern times hardly known. Although Willie was highly respected by all, he was not the center of attention at the Danse Calinda. A striking woman named Maman Rara was. Willie told me that in the 1940's Hollywood had made a picture about her called *"Macumba Love."* Maman Rara was about 5'9" and solid, with a fierce; orange gaze, red-brick complexion and a mane of white hair as thick and luxuriant as a waterfall. Her helper was a tall, bald, beige complexioned man of thin frame and delicate features, his name was Maitre Baptiste. Although Maman Rara had not a wrinkle, she gave the impression of possessing great age. When a conga drum began to be heard and a guitar joined it, a soft song rose from the throats of the 35 or-so people gathered:

> *"Danse calinda boudum boudum, Danse calinda dum, Danse calinda boudum boudum Maman Rara Bomba henen henen, Rara Bomba henen.* "

With legs wide apart and arms akimbo, Maman Rara began to dance in a hypnotic, rhythmic fashion. It was sort of a march, sort of a calypso, but whatever it was, it was preternaturally beautiful. I watched with the others as this woman of great age transformed herself into the most desirable creature I had ever seen. Without warning, she grabbed a cat by its tail, smashed it against a tree, and dropped it into a waiting cauldron full of boiling water. Everyone then began to scream; I became apprehensive. For the first time I felt extremely uncomfortable. Maman Rara then grabbed a black rooster, broke its legs and wings, and left it by the tree, still alive. As one who had been trained in Santería to sacrifice animals in a humane fashion, I was not comfortable with this style of sacrifice where the animal was made to suffer. Willie later told me that the breaking of the bird's legs and wings is symbolic of the material plane, where mankind's spiritual potential is stifled by the crippling effects of the flesh. It was also symbolic of slavery, where a human being was spiritually and emotionally crippled, the slave's "wings" and "legs" being broken by the scourge of the master. Willie also told me that tormenting the animals before sacrificing them causes their remains to be supercharged with powerful energy, very useful when doing works of an offensive nature.

According to Willie, Maman Rara, who was his cousin and also a direct descendant of the mythic Marie Laveau, was the latest in a long line of Voodoo queens, the greatest of whom was Mamzelle, as those close to Marie Laveau called her.

"Before you learns to make gris-gris you gots to know about Mamzelle, boy," Willie would tell me. "There ain't no Noo O-lEEns Voodoo without her. Like the old song goes, *Marie Laveau est Voudou, et Voudou est Marie Laveau.*"

According to Willie, the greatest secret any magician in any tradition can learn is that magic doesn't stop outside the rituals and ceremonies designed to invoke invisible powers; magic is whatever works. One of Marie Laveau's most renowned miracles, her famous eleventh-hour saving of condemned men, may have had more to do with earthly influence than with supernatural power, but that fact doesn't detract one bit from her standing as a great magician.

Before becoming a Voodoo queen, Marie was a famous hairdresser. In New Orleans during the early 19th century, society women did not go to beauty salons to have their hair done. They would employ the services of certain women of color who would come to their houses, to coiff their hair in the latest, intricate, fashions. As a celebrated hairdresser, Marie was making a fairly good living by the time she was in her mid-twenties. Then as now, women gossiped with their hairdressers. In fact, an astute young woman like Marie could become an amateur psychiatrist, encouraging her clients to pour their hearts out to her. Early on, Marie began to understand that information can be a powerful weapon. It appears that Marie was doing the hair of the wife of an extremely powerful man when the woman confessed to her that she and her husband enjoyed sharing their bed with their slave, an extremely tall and handsome Senegalese who behind closed doors was the real master of the household, since both the woman and the man were serviced sexually by him.

While doing the hair of a woman who belonged to an old and noble family, but had limited assets, Marie heard a story that was to change her life. The woman was disconsolate because her son was to be hanged for having murdered his girlfriend, whom he caught cuckolding with a colored servant.

"Oh, Marie, I'd give anything to save my son, but I don't have enough money to buy the judges. I've spent every dollar I had on Voodoos who've taken my money and given me nothing in return. And to top it all off, the judge in charge of the case, Pierre Deveraux, has the reputation of being incorruptible."

At the mention of the name Deveraux, Marie's eyes lit up. Madame Devoreaux was Marie's client, the one whose husband was "serviced" by the Senegalese slave.

"I can save your son, Madame, but what would you give me in return?"

Somewhat skeptical, but desperate enough to grasp at straws, the woman said:

"I have no money left, but I own a nice small house on St. Anne street that has been in my family for many years. If you save my son, the house is yours," the woman told Marie.

Immediately, Marie spoke to Madame Devoreaux, telling that her husband the judge had committed a grave offense by condemning a young man who had committed a crime of passion to die in the gallows. Marie let it be known that if the judge did not obtain a pardon for the young man, his peculiar relationship with the Senegalese slave would be widely known. Indignant, the woman asked Marie,

"And what makes you think anyone would believe a lowly servant like you?"

To which she replied,

"I am not so presumptuous as to believe that my colored lips would be heard over those white ones of yours, Madame, but the young man's mother's lips are as white as yours, and her name just as honorable. I've left an envelope with her to hold and be opened only if something happens to me, or if I tell her to open it. In it I describe your situation, and I'm sure she'll move hell and high water to make sure the judge's peculiar habits are known."

By the time of the Decoreaux affair, Marie had begun a practice of selling love charms and other medicines in a low-key way to her customers. She had begun to learn Voodoo from the fabled Dr. John at about this time also, so Marie saw all of the events that converged as proof that she was meant to be a great "Voodooienne." Judge Devoreaux called Marie to his chambers.

"What do you want from me?"

"I know the governor is in town for Mardi Gras. He is your brother-in-law, you can easily talk him into offering the young man a pardon. He is a white aristocrat without prior offenses, a perfect candidate for a pardon."

"Alright, Marie, you can count on it. Anything else?"

"As a matter of fact, yes, I don't want the pardon to be given until the young man is actually at the gallows, with the noose around his neck."

And so it was that Marie told the young man's mother that her spirits would intercede for the young man at the eleventh hour. When this actually happened, Marie Laveau not only found herself proprietor of her own house, but also was immediately transformed from a successful hairdresser into the most powerful force in New Orleans Voodoo.

Marie Laveau was born in 1794, but no one is sure where. Willie says she was born in the vicinity of New Orleans. The first public record still available mentioning Marie Laveau is that of her marriage, in the archives of St. Louis Cathedral. The contract reads as follows:

Paris, Jacques,
a free Quarteroon, illegitimate,
a native of Jeremias, Ste. Domingue,
son of Jacques Paris and Blou Samitte,
married Laveau, Marie,
a native of New Orleans,
illegitimate daughter of
Charles Laveau and Marguerite Darcantel,
August 4, 1819.

The ceremony was performed by the saintly and celebrated priest Pere Antoine, a beloved figure in New Orleans history who, at his death in 1829 was to lie in state for three days while hundreds of thousands Orleanians filed by his frail body to pay last respects. Marie had been very dedicated to Pere Antoine, and while the priest lived, she had kept her involvement with Voodoo secret and was, in fact, extremely active in church affairs, being the most prominent volunteer of the parish, distinguishing herself by tending to yellow fever victims as well as prisoners.

At the time of the Paris-Laveau marriage, Voodoo was thriving in New Orleans. The "Big Three" of Voodoo were Dr. John, Sanite Dede, and Marie Saloppe. Dr. John was a big, striking, black man who came from Cuba and quickly became a powerful figure in New Orleans because of his vast knowledge of magic. Dr. John's entire face was decorated with scars, indicative of his royal standing in his native Senegal. After he bought his freedom in Cuba, he went back to Senegal to find his people, but discovered that he no longer liked living in Africa. Eventually, Dr. John, then known as Juan Montana, ended up in New Orleans, where he soon became a wealthy practitioner of Voodoo, owning fifteen slaves himself, all of them women. Dr. John dressed extravagantly, rode in a carriage as fine as that of the Governor, and counted among his clients aristocrats and politicians. Under his guidance Voodoo became an accepted and organized part of New Orleans life. So many important people patronized Dr. John, that he was practically immune to prosecution for any crime he may have committed. Although Dr. John had a well-known hatred for mixed race people, calling his own children by white women "mules," he seems to have recognized in Marie Laveau a kindred magical spirit, for he took her under his wing and trained her to be a Voodoo queen. It was from Dr. John that Marie learned the value of having informants

DOCTOR JOHN

everywhere. When Marie started to gain fame as a hairdresser, Dr. John instructed her to put at least one servant in each household under his pay as a spy. When Dr. John became too old to maintain his empire. Marie was prepared to take his place.

It seems as if Jacques Paris did not stay with Marie long, for a newspaper clipping of 1821 mentioning Marie's coiffure of the queen of Mardi Gras referred to her as "the Widow Paris," even though Jacques Paris was still alive then. By this time, Marie had also met the man of her life, one Louis Christophe Duminy de Glapion who, like Paris, had been a refugee from Sainte Domingue. 1830 seems to have been a banner year for Marie Laveau. Since Pere Antoine's recent death, Marie had become much more open about her practice of Voodoo. After she moved to the house in St. Anne, clients began to come to her in droves. Shrewd and extremely intelligent, Marie assessed the situation of Voodoo at the time and saw an opportunity to move in at the top. The religion was not organized, there were many women calling themselves "queens," and only three really strong competitors for the new upstart: Sanite Dede, Marie Saloppe, and the still formidable Dr. John. Dr. John had reigned for almost a century and was ready to move over, Sanite disappeared under mysterious circumstances, and Marie Saloppe accepted a position as an underling or minor queen under Marie Laveau. All other "queens" were either forced to swear allegiance to Laveau or they were unceremoniously made to leave town. By the end of 1830 Marie Laveau was the undisputed queen of New Orleans Voodoo and one of the most powerful women in America.

Willie tells me Marie quietly married Glapion after Paris died, but she continued to call herself "the Widow Paris." By 1835, when Glapion also died, Marie was at the peak of her power, as indicated by the relatively prominent funeral notice posted by the New Orleans Daily Picayune of June 17, 1835:

> *Died yesterday, at one o'clock,*
> *at the age of 66 years*
> *Christophe Duminy Glapion*
> *His friends and acquaintances*
> *are invited to attend his funeral,*
> *without any other invitation,*
> *which will take place this evening*
> *at precisely five; o'clock.*
> *The funeral will leave from his home,*
> *St. Anne between Burgundy and Rampart Sts.*

Largely because of Marie's fame, Glapion's funeral drew great crowds. The mayor and the chief of police showed up, as well as many other city and state officials.

Marie owned several houses in the vicinity of her own, as well as a famous structure called "La Maison Blanche" on the outskirts of New Orleans, in the town of Milneburg. This house served as a gathering place for the more serious *"Voodoos"* as well as a *"house of assignations"* where wealthy white gentlemen could meet in private with young quadroon women.

According to Willie, the legend that Marie Laveau was immortal and possessed the secret of eternal youth was perpetrated by Marie herself with the help of her daughter, called "Ti Marie." Although Marie Laveau looked remarkably young for her age in 1869, she was over seventy years old and wanted to slow down her pace. The brilliant ruse she played on everyone worked so well that to this day there is confusion as to where the truth lies. It seems that Marie, in front of everybody, said she was going to receive a rejuvenating blessing from Papa Limba/St. Peter himself. Dressed with a blue turban and a yellow dress, she went into a small hut by Pontchartrain Lake while her followers sang and danced for three days in a row. At the end of the three days, a remarkably rejuvenated Marie emerged wearing her blue turban and yellow dress.

In reality, Marie Laveau arranged to have her daughter take her place, pretending to be her, while she retired quietly to the Maison Blanche, from then on made off limits to everyone. Marie Leveau lived her last days in quiet contemplation, while her daughter continued to live the life of her Marie Laveau, Voodoo queen, until the death of her mother in 1881. Ti Marie was forty-two when she took over for her mother (apparently she had been occasionally substituting for her mother, understudying the character "Marie Laveau," since the 1850's). So striking was the resemblance between mother and daughter that, according to Willie, even family members were fooled. Willie said that, for all intents and purposes, mother and daughter were the same entity. Two persons and one true essence.

Upon Marie's death in 1881 a curious thing happened, Ti Marie was never heard from again. Apparently, an older daughter of Marie Leveau, one Madame Legendre, who looked white and was married to a white man, took over ownership of the St. Ann street cottage and decided to put the Marie Laveau legend to rest by banishing Ti Marie to the Maison Blanche. How she managed to do this is not clear. One rumor has it that Ti Marie and Madame Legendre were one and the same. At any rate, the death of Marie Laveau marked the effective end of the public life of Ti Marie, although she apparently continued to rule the Voodoos from her exile in the Maison Blanche for several more years.

Like any great entrepreneurial leader, Marie Laveau had many sources of income. She organized weekly Voodoo dances at Congo Square and Lake Pontchartrain that were very successful. At a time when a dollar could buy you a night at a fine hotel, she was charging ten dollars per person to those who wanted to attend these dances. She also rented out apartments, bungalows, and houses all over the French Quarter. Marie also handled the delicate liaisons between white gentleman and young quadroon women, many of such meetings taking place at the Maison Blanche. Marie also managed a dozen lesser "Voodoo queens," including her former mentor, Marie Saloppe, and had a thriving practice as a Voodoo priestess/fortune teller herself. Most of her income derived from selling gris-gris bags, juju bags, and mojo bags. The word "gris" is French for "gray," appropriate designation for an amoral magic that is neither black nor white.

Most of all, Marie was eclectic and would do whatever it took to get her way, as was the case when another quadroon named Rosalie set herself up as a rival of Marie's. For a time, Rosalie created quite a stir. This was 1850 and Marie had reigned over the Voodoos with an iron grip for over twenty years. Rosalie's power derived from a wooden sculpture said to have been a West African deity brought from the old country. This fantastic looking statue was for awhile the talk of the town. One day, Marie simply walked into Rosalie's place when she wasn't there and just walked away with the statue. Rosalie complained to the police, who sent an officer, watchman Ferdinand Abreau, to confiscate the deity until the matter could be resolved in the courts. An item in the Daily Picayune of July 3, 1850, read thus:

> ## CURIOUS CHARGE OF SWINDLING
> Marie Laveaux [(sic)], otherwise Widow Paris, the head of the Voudou women, yesterday appeared before Recorder Seuzenean and charged Watchman Abreau with having by fraud come into possession of a statue of a "virgin", worth $50.

This was no doubt the deity in question. As usual, the courts sided with Marie, giving her possession of the "virgin," in exchange for $8.50 in court costs. After Marie obtained ownership of the statue, Rosalie was never heard from again.

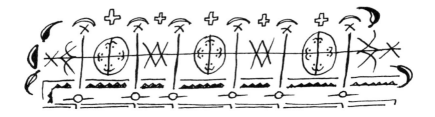

2

A Gris-Gris
for Every Occasion

Generally speaking, "mojo" works were considered "white magic," amulets to attract good luck and love. "Juju" "ouanga" "hexes" and other evil works are called "black magic." Marie Laveau taught that "gris-gris," gray magic, was a combination of both, for what is good for you may not necessarily be good for the guy standing next to you! The gris-gris which follow were all instituted by Marie Laveau herself and have been kept in her line as a precious legacy from a magnificent sorceress.

"HEX-PROOFING" YOUR HOME
NEW ORLEANS STYLE

Orlenians since before the time of Marie Laveau swear by the power of red brick dust to ward off evil. Simply get an old red brick, hammer it to dust, and spread the dust around the front of your house, using a broom. Keep a pan of water that has been treated with a ball of Indigo blueing *(añil)* behind your front door, and draw crosses using cascarilla behind every door of the house. Add a couple of drops of urine from a child and use the mixture as a floor wash, this will complete making your home hex-proof.

GAMBLING GRIS-GRIS

Ingredients

- *A piece of chamois*   - *A piece of red flannel*
- *A Shark's tooth*   - *Sap from a Pine tree*
- *Blood from a pigeon*

1. Mix the blood and sap together.
2. Write amount you wish to win on the piece of chamois with the mixture.
3. Place the shark's tooth on top, then some cat hair. Cover with red flannel.
4. Sew red flannel to chamois using black thread, trapping everything inside.
5. Wear on left shoe.

ANOTHER GAMBLING CHARM

A powerful gambling charm is made by placing the following items in a leather bag:

- *A bone from a black cat*   - *A bat's heart*
- *High John the Conqueror root*   - *Ginger root*
- *Two lodestones with plenty of iron filings.*

Anoint your bag with Luck at Gambling oil every week and carry the bag on your left pocket when you play.

MAKE A MISER GIVE UP HIS MONEY

Bathe in a tub half filled with water into which a box of borax, 5 Cinnamon sticks, and 1/2 cup of sugar has been added. Meet the miser right after taking the bath, he'll spend his last cent on you.

TO BRING CUSTOMERS TO A SHOP

Use ammonia, nutmeg, and sugar in the water used to scrub the shop. Pour a little whiskey in all four corners, customers will beat a path to your door.

TO WIN A COURT CASE

1. Write names of judge and each member of the jury, as well as the name of the prosecuting attorney, on a piece of parchment.

2. Fold paper so it can fit a hole drilled on a large block of ice. After inserting paper in the hole fill it in with powdered sugar.

3. Arrange nine white candles around the block of ice and rap nine times on the floor while saying:

   "Just Judge, save _____ *"*
   nine times.

TO MAKE SOMEONE
WHO HAS LEFT YOU COME BACK

Burn the clothes of the one who left in a pan with some chicken droppings.

ANOTHER ONE TO
WIN A COURT CASE

1. Write all the witnesses' names on a piece of parchment. Slice into a beef tongue so that you can place the parchment inside.

2. Tie the tongue with a black cord to hold the parchment in place.

3. Take a lit black candle, a lit cigar, and salt, place along with prepared tongue on top of dish and put dish on top of a block of ice.

4. You then put name of judge and district attorney in a mixture of nine lumps of sugar, honey, strawberry syrup, and Come-to-Me oil.

5. Mix all this and light a yellow candle in the middle of it, then ask your spirit guides to help you.

When both candles have burned, leave everything by the courthouse without being seen.

TO MAKE TWO PEOPLE GET MARRIED

1. Take St. Joseph's picture and put sand in front of it.

2. Write the couple's names in the sand and light twelve pink candles around the picture and the name in a circle.

3. Get a male doll and a female doll and tie their hands together using a white satin ribbon, then place them in the center of the circle.

4. Pray to St., Joseph to make this happen, then put some parsley and cooked macaroni in the center of the circle as an offering.

TO KEEP YOUR BOSS FROM FIRING YOU

Write his name on a piece of paper and bury it in your backyard with a chopped-up red candle and a black cat's tail.

TO KEEP A LOVER FAITHFUL

Get a bit of Black Devil Oil, mix with sugar and salt, and sprinkle a little on your lover's underwear. She or he won't mess around with anyone else but you!

- or -

The old "Marie Laveau trick" to keep men faithful consists of feeding him your bodily fluids, especially your menstrual blood. This procedure is common in Cuban Santería and may have been taught to Laveau by her first Voodoo teacher, Doctor John, who came to Louisiana from Senegal via Cuba, where he became a powerful Santero.

TO GET BACK AT AN ENEMY

Ingredients

1 oz. Saffron • 1 Tsp. salt • 1 Tsp. gunpowder • A little bit of dry, pulverized dog shit

Melt a black candle, use wax to form a ball with all of the ingredients. Throw ball in your enemy's property, preferably where he won't see it, such as under his house.

TO MAKE SOMEONE SICK

1. Write name of the person you wish to harm on a piece of parchment.

2. Melt half a black candle, making a ball with the molten wax by kneading and rolling it around the written name so the name is trapped inside the ball of wax.

3. Place the ball in a tub of very hot water. Sit by the tub and, using a stick, toss and turn it for at least six hours. The person whose name is inside the wax ball will become violently ill.

FOR SPRAINS AND SWELLINGS

Ingredients

Hot water • Epsom salts • Whiskey • Candles

Apply a compress made out of hot water, Epsom salt, and whiskey to affected area. Light a candle to appropriate deity or spirit, for example, St. Lazarus if an infection, to St. Barbara if you were injured by lightning, to Oshun if you have stomach problems.

TO GET RID OF A PERSON

Write name of the person who you want to get rid of on a red balloon filled with helium. Light a yellow candle to St. Expedito on a Thursday, and let the balloon go. Your enemy will go the way the air takes the balloon.

MAKE A PERSON CHANGE HIS MIND

1. Burn three black candles for half an hour, then melt them.

2. Write person's name four times backwards and five times forward on a scrap of silk, put into wax.

3. Throw lump under his house.

4. Next, write his name once on another piece of silk. Open a small hole in coconut, insert name, add honey and sugar to the coconut, then, using your right foot, roll the coconut from the back to the front of the house repeating over and over:

"Your head is hard as a coconut, but you're going to change your mind!"

- or -

1. On a piece of parchment, in Dove's Blood ink, write the name of the person whose mind you want to change nine times.

2. Wrap the parchment around a licorice stick, wrap a red ribbon nine feet in length tightly around the parchment.

3. Bury it near the person's home under cover of darkness. By the end of the fourth day after the burial, you will notice a desired change in the person whose mind you wished to change.

TO FIGHT IMPOTENCY

Dried testicles of a black cat, worn on a leather bag near your own genitals, will make you hard as a rock.

TO ATTRACT SOMEONE ELSE'S MATE

If you should fall in love with the mate of a friend, this potent charm, created by Marie Laveau, is said to destroy the marriage. You in turn will then be the sole object of his or her affections. Blend the following ingredients:

Ingredients

Tonka Bean	*1 bean*
Damiana Powder	*1/2 teaspoon*
Come to Me Powder	*1 teaspoon*
7 Powers Incense	*2 teaspoons*

1. Thoroughly mix all of the ingredients and mix into a half glass of red wine. Allow to soak for 24 hours.

2. Anoint yourself with this potent liquid before leaving the house. Make the sign of the cross with some of this mixture on your forehead, chest, tops of both hands and on your feet.

3. Sprinkle yourself with 3 drops of Compelling Oil.

4. Dust your genital area with Come to Me Powder.

5. Do all of these things for 21 consecutive days. After the twenty-first day, take the rest of the liquid and sprinkle it around the outer edge of your front door. The person you so strongly desire as a lover will be compelled to come and offer you love and happiness.

Marie Laveau received fantastic sums of money over the years for her services in concocting just such charms as above. She would never accept less than $10 when anyone asked her for assistance this was enough to have your fortune told and to obtain a small good luck charm or *gris gris* designed especially for whatever purpose you had in mind. Marie did much work in the area of sex during her 40 year span of rule as High Priestess in New Orleans. When an affair was wanted by someone, she charged in accordance with how wealthy a patron was and what they could afford. This type activity usually ran between $50 and $1000.

TO INCREASE YOUR SEXUAL CHARM

Ingredients

Pimento Powder	*1 teaspoon*
Bayberry Incense	*1/2 cup*
Orchid (crushed)	*1/2 cup*
Frankincense Powder	*1/4 cup*
Dill	*1/4 cup*

Blend all of the above ingredients in a wooden bowl, cover tightly, and set aside in a cool dark place until needed. It is to be burned on Fast Lighting Charcoal. Burn a small amount of the mixture just before your loved one is due home, and also burn more while in the throes of passionate lovemaking. Your lover will appreciate you more fully as a result of this, and he or she will cease having sexual relations with others.

LOVE GRIS-GRIS

Place the following items in a small bag and sleep with it under your pillow:

- *Personal effect of person to be "worked"*
- *Steel dust • Honey • Sugar*

WHEN SEXUAL DESIRE FOR
SOMEONE IS A SECRET

The following ingredients are to be carefully blended. When finished, place the mixture in a red flannel bag and tightly tie the top together. Attach a white cotton string and wear around your neck. Within 7 days your wish for a new sexual partner will be fulfilled.

Ingredients

Camphor Powder	*1/2 teaspoon*
Frankincense	*1 teaspoon*
Myrrh Incense	*A pinch*
Orris Root Powder	*1/4 teaspoon*
Patchouly Leaves (ground)	*A pinch*
Sandalwood Incense	*1/4 teaspoon*
Saltpeter	*3/4 teaspoon*

If you do not obtain a new lover within the 7 day period, empty the sack. Burn a small amount of the mixture each morning for 7 straight days. You will unexpectedly meet and make passionate love with someone.

FOR A GIRL TO ATTRACT A LOVER

Follow these instructions for nine consecutive nights. Use the juice of four lemons to rub your legs and the posts of your bed.. Put a glass of water under your bed, lie with your knees bent up and your legs spread wide until you fall asleep. On the ninth night, a man of worth will come your way.

TO BREAK UP A COUPLE

Mix the following ingredients and throw on the front steps of either or both targeted people.

- *Cayenne Pepper*
- *A Bluestone*
- *Mud from a wasp's nest*
- *Dragon's Blood incense*
- *Gunpowder*
- *BB shots*
- *Flaxseed*
- *Filé*

WORKS DONE WITH FOUR THIEVES VINEGAR

Legend has it that during the days of the European plague in the 14th century, four thieves who were looting the dead bodies discovered a potion to ward off disease. Although this powerful ingredient is a fairly common item in occult stores and Voodoo shops, it may not be available where you live. Here is the way it is usually made in New Orleans.

Ingredients

- *1 gallon cider vinegar*
- *1 oz. rosemary*
- *1 oz. wormwood*
- *1 oz. lavender*
- *1 oz. pwdr. camphor*
- *1 oz. sage*
- *1 oz. peppermint*
- *1 oz. lemongrass*
- *1 oz. rue*

Mix everything inside tightly-closed glass container, heat by placing container in boiling water for four minutes each of four days, beginning on a Monday. On the fourth day, strain the solids out and bottle your homemade Four Thieves Vinegar.

TO MAKE SOMEONE MOVE AWAY

Dampen doorknob of the front door of the person you want to move away with Four Thieves Vinegar while visualizing his or her departure, this will make him or her want to get as far away from as possible.

TO TIE YOUR LOVER TO YOU

Measure his erect penis using a string, then tie nine knots on the string and always carry it with you. He'll only be able to achieve an erection when he is with you.

CALINDA UNHEXING BATH

Ingredients

- *1 head of Garlic*
- *3 leaves of Sage*
- *Geranium water*
- *Dry Basil*
- *1 bunch of Parsley*
- *1 teaspoon Saltpeter*

Bathe in this on Monday, Wednesday, and Friday. Rub your body with Bay Rum afterwards, then with Vervain oil and Honeysuckle oil. No evil thing can penetrate one who has bathed in the Calinda Unhexing Bath.

TO SUBJUGATE A MALE LOVER

After he ejaculates inside you, take a towel, wipe yourself with it and, while he sleeps, wave it on top of him while saying:

"lambeh yoh du su., je peu mais qu'tu!"
This will make him gentle and docile.

TO HEX SOMEONE

1. Wet a piece of parchment in Four Thieves Vinegar then let it dry.

2. Write name of person you wish to hex using Dragon's Blood ink.

3. Hold the paper in the flame of a Black candle which has been dressed with Damnation powder and Patchouli oil.

4. Sprinkle resulting ashes by your enemy's place of residence. Your enemy's existence will be made into a living hell.

TO DEFEAT AN ENEMY

To a cup of salt, add 4 ounces of Four Thieves Vinegar. Sprinkle by your enemy's house or by a path he will cross. This will assure your victory and his utter defeat.

- or -

Light a Brown candle in the middle of a bowl filled with sugar to which three teaspoonfuls of Four Thieves Vinegar has been added before going to bed, the next day, take what's left of the candle and the sugar and throw it in your enemy's yard.

TO DRIVE SOMEONE MAD

Prepare a soup with plenty of fresh vegetables and a rat. Whoever eats this soup will go crazy.

KILLING SPELLS

There's no doubt about it. If a client came to Marie Laveau with $500.00 asking her to "hoodoo " someone to death, she would consider doing the dreadful deed provided that three conditions were met 1) The person had to deserve it 2) Marie's guardian spirits had to OK the "hit. " and 3) Money was to be paid in advance, with no guarantees about the results.

• Write victim's name on parchment using Dragon's Blood, put it inside a fish with lots of black pepper, sew fish up, then bury fish in victim's backyard. Victim will die within 13 days.

• Another one is to put their name inside a cow's heart along with some strong tobacco, bury it near where the victim lives.

• Catch a rattlesnake, kill it and hang it by the sun to dry, put a piece of parchment with the person's name written on it inside the snake's mouth. As the snake dries up and withers, the person slowly dies.

• Kill a rooster, chop off its head and feet and take them to a graveyard. Put a black candle in the rooster's beak, lay it down in front of a tomb and bury the feet in the back of the tomb. Light the candle and pray for one hour that the person is destroyed. Then dig up the feet and take them, along with the head, to the person's backyard. Bury them there, the person won't last a week.

MARIE LAVEAU'S GOOFER DUST

Ingredients

*• Dirt from nine graves of nine criminals,
preferably hanged or executed men
• 1 teaspoon of gunpowder   • Dried pigeon shit.
• Black pepper   • A live Rooster*

1. During Holy Friday, at midnight, go to a deserted crossroads with your ingredients, get stark naked while smoking a cigar, spill some rum while calling Papa Legba to bless your efforts.

2. Leave three coin dollars in the crossroads, along with a rooster you decapitate right there.

3. Grab some dirt from the crossroads, add to ingredients, mix them all up and save in a red bag.

4. As you leave the spot, don't look back! You have produced one of the most feared Voodoo ingredients.

Contrary to popular belief, Goofer Dust is not used solely for evil purposes. It also has powerful protective qualities when mixed with ingredients that are used for positive purposes.

CEMETERY DIRT FOR PROTECTION

Besides goofer dust, cemetery dirt is an important ingredient in many charms, gris-gris, Elegguas, and other African-derived charms and amulets. A popular protection against evil is a gris-gris consisting of a small cloth bag filledwith a flower from a friend or loved one's funeral, a pebble found in the cemetery the day of his/her burial, and some dirt from his/her grave site. Pour some holy water on the whole thing and carry the bag with you for protection against enemies.

3

From the Notebooks
of Marie Laveau...

Willie Glapion held as his most treasured possessions a trio of yellowed, worn-out notebooks he said his father copied and had translated from those of Marie Laveau herself, in possession of Marie's great-granddaughter, Willie's mom. Willie's father, the Rev. Willie Johnston, was a black preacher who left the church to live with Willie's mother, Elise Glapion, known as "Queen Lala," a very light skinned quadroon. Apparently, the reverend, who spoke no Creole, had the notebooks translated so that his woman wouldn't be able to put one over him. This suited Willie fine, since he didn't speak much Creole either. I only had opportunity to copy from the treasured artifacts a couple of times, what follows is what I was able to gleam from the fabled coheirs.

Marie Laveau apparently wrote these notebooks as *"how to"* manuals intended to teach her students the business side of Voodoo, including how to manufacture most of the lucrative oils, candles, and powders of the trade, and also how much to charge. The $500.00 she said should be charged for a death spell *"provided they deserve it,"* and the $5,000 charged for saving someone from the hangman gives an idea of how lucrative Marie's business was. Remember these are 1875 dollars! I guess a dollar in New Orleans in 1875 would buy you what a hundred dollars buys you today.

MARIE LAVEAU'S
SECRET RECIPES

Here, for the first time, find the contents of exotic Voodoo oils and powders.

BLACK CAT OIL: To a can of machine oil, pray "Our Father" backwards at midnight, light a black candle. In the morning, it has become "Black Cat Oil."

BRIMSTONE: Sulfur

LOVE OIL: Olive oil, gardenia oil.

MAGNETIC VINEGAR: Cider vinegar; two lodestones. Magnetic Vinegar is used to fight influenza, distemper, consumption, and fever. Put two lodestones inside a bottle of vinegar, recite the words *"Sour, hour, vinegar, V! Keep the sickness off of me!"* over the bottle. Instruct clients to make a cross on their foreheads thrice per day. Dip a white chicken feather in the vinegar and sell as anti-influenza amulet.

CONTROLLING POWDER: Corn starch, Saltpeter & Epsom salt

DRAWING POWDER: Corn meal, confectioner's sugar.

FLYING DEVIL OIL: 8 Oz. olive oil, red food coloring, 1 Oz. red cayenne pepper.

Follow Me Water: Water, two drops of honey, one cinnamon stick, 1 female John the Conqueror, and two drops of your urine.

Love Perfume: Florida Water, Rose water, Cinnamon powder, honey.

JOHNNY THE CONQUEROR ROOT

There are three different kinds, Big male John, Big female John, and Little John. This root works best for males. It makes women do whatever their men want!

> *"I don't work with no female John. You can always tell the male 'cause of its longer point and rough skin."*

IF A WOMAN ISN'T TREATING HER MAN RIGHT, all he has to do is put some "Johnny Come To Me" under her bed. This is done by mixing some big John [(High John the Conqueror)], sugar, and cayenne pepper. Up to $25.00 [(1875)] dollars can be charged for this work.

IF A WOMAN IS CHEATING, have her man put some High John in her pillow, she'll never cheat again.

"Johnny Commanding" powder is used to MAKE SOMEONE A SLAVE. Have client blow this powder directly on his victim's back, or pour powder in front of his house, where he'll step. To make Johnny Commanding, mix some High John with goofer dust and red brick dust, that's all.

A SURE-FIRE WAY TO GET A WOMAN TO BE A MAN'S SLAVE is to get her to hold a piece of High John while he is making love to her.

"Johnny Attracting Oil" is made by putting a piece of High John in a bottle of olive oil. After a few days, the root becomes very powerful and should be sold at a very high price. If a client places this root under the steps in front of his intended's house, she'll fall for him like a child.

As a bag *for men to be attractive to women,* soak a nice big piece of High John in sugar water for 24 hours, then put root inside red flannel bag. This will make any man attractive.

Sell a bag containing a piece of "Big John" to a man who plays the dice, tell him to keep it in his back pocket and to touch his thumb to it when throwing. He'll win.

NO-FAIL SPELL TO GET
A PARTICULAR WOMAN

If your client knows the name of the woman he wants, tell him to tell you and prepare the following gris-gris for him:

1. Take a grapefruit, cut it in half and place one half on a pie plate.

2. Put nine pink birthday cake candles all around the half grapefruit.

3. Add to center of fruit some cayenne pepper, Epsom salt, sugar, and salt, write woman's name on piece of paper and stick it inside grapefruit.

4. Tell client to walk around in a nine-foot circle, clockwise, carrying pie plate with everything on it, including lit candles. Also, rub a piece of High John while doing this.

Tell client to do this for nine days
and the gal will be his.

LODESTONES: Always sell them in pairs, one piece drives away evil, the other brings good luck. They should be placed in chamois bags and fed every six months with either magnetic sand, which is made of pulverized lodestones, or iron filings.

FIVE FINGERS GRASS: This is a good protection amulet to sell the curious, for it is beneficial, good, and cheap for us to get, since it grows all over. Each of the fingers carries a special blessing from Papa Bondieu:

1) Luck   2) Money
3) Power   4) Wisdom   5) Love

This herb should be hung upside down over the bed to get sleep that is free from evil.

MARIE LAVEAU'S FAMOUS TALISMANS

Marie Laveau was famous for her talismans, which she mostly called "gris-gris." These potent charms usually consisted of a simplified ve-ve drawn with either animal blood or an organic ink such as Dragon's Blood on parchment. The parchment would then be sewn into a small bag made of red flannel, green flannel, or black leather. Marie's clients spent thousands of dollars on these charms and they swore by them. On the following pages we present several of Marie Laveau's wonderful talismans.

Marie Leveau
for
Protection

Lwa La Sirene
for
Seduction of the Opposite Sex

Lwa Damballah
for
Wealth & Luck

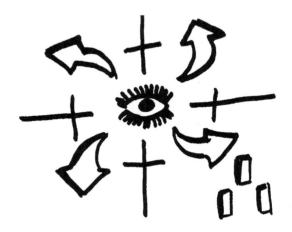

Lwa Aida Niedo
for
Gaing Control of Your Future

Lwa Onzoncire
will make you
Strong-Willed

Lwa Marie
for
Winning Court Cases

Lwa Bossu-Trois-Cornes
for
Protection from Accidents

Lwa Marinette
for
Protection from Ilness

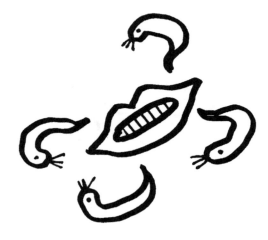

Lwa Ezili-Freda-Dahomey
for
Sexual Potency

Lwa Gran-Bois
for
Clarity of Mind

Lwa Kalfu
for
Protection when Traveling

Lwa Ursule
for
Females to Dominate Males

Lwa Ogu
for
Power and Wisdom

4

Create Your Own
Mojo, Gris-Gris and Ouanga Bags

What differentiates a client from a practitioner is not only initiation, but attitude. In New Orleans Voodoo, there are numerous cases of self-initiated practitioners who became famous. Unlike Cuban Santería and Haitian Vodou, where "apostolic" succession -- bona fide initiation from a recognized initiate representing an ancient lineage is supremely important. New Orleans Voodoo is like Wicca in its eclectic approach to initiation and practice. Mojo, gris-gris, and ouanga bags, collectively called "conjure bags," can be made by the uninitiated once he or she has received enough "mojo" (ashé, power) from his/her guardian spirits to effect efficacious charms and talismans. When making these bags, trust in your instincts and follow some basic guidelines. There will probably be some trial and error mistakes you'll make, but in the end, you'll emerge more powerful and satisfied at having won the capability of manipulating the natural forces around you to your benefit, the mark of a true magician. Personally, I can't imagine how I could have gotten to where I am, magically, without the guidance of my teachers, but for those who think they can teach themselves; good luck! Use your common sense, intuition, and spirit guides to assemble these bags.

Conjure bags should contain no more than 13 and no less than 3 ingredients, and never even numbers. While I'll give you here the ingredients Marie Laveau used in her bags, you may intuitively add your own once you get the hang of conjure-bag making. Remember that conjure bags operate mainly on the principle of imitative magic - *like produces like* - so if you want see a couple separated, you may cut a photograph of the couple in half, separating them in the world-writ-small, which through the power of the superior will of the magician, causes the same effect in the world-writ-largem the actual separation of the couple!

Always ask your spirit guides and deities for guidance and protection before you start; offering a candle (fire), water, incense (air), and flowers (earth) to them in whatever ritual is appropriate for you.

INGREDIENTS FOR LOVE BAGS
(usually made out of red flannel)

Adam and Eve root
Alexandrine
Allspice
Amber
Apricot
Aquamarine
Arrowhead
Balm of Gilead
Basil
Beth root
Bleeding Heart
Bluestones*

Cardemon
Catnip
Cayenne
Chamomille
Chrysocoile
Cinnamon
Clove
Clover
Columbine
Copal
Coral
Coriander

* Most powerful on Wednesdays

Crocus
Cubeb berries
Daffodil
Daisy
Damiana
Diamond
Dill
Elecampane
Elm
Emerald
Endive
Fig
Flowers from a wedding
Gardenia
Geranium
Ginger
Heart of a swallow
Hibiscus
High John the Conqueror
Hyacinth
Indian paintbrush
Jade
Jasmine
Juniper
Key
Lady's mantle
Lapis
Laurel
Lavender
Lemon balm
Lemon vervain
Lepidolite
Linden
Lodestones (two)
Lovage

Maidenhair fern
Malachite
Mandrake
Maple
Marjoram
Myrtle
Moonstone
Nutmeg
Olive
Onyx
Opal
Orange blossoms
Orchid
Orris root
Oshun**
Pansy
Peach
Pearl
Peppermint
Periwinkle
Poppy
Primrose
Pink candle
Pink quartz
Rhodochrosite
Rose
Rosemary
Rue
Ruby
Saffron
Sapphire
Shango**
Skullcap
Southernwood
Spearmint

*** Oil, Candle, Incense, or Image*

Spiderwort
Strawberry
Shells
Thyme
Tonka bean
Topaz
Tourmaline, pink
Tulip

Turquoise
Vanilla
Vervain
Violet
Willow
Wedding ring
Wood betony
Yarrow

INGREDIENTS FOR
LUCKY/GAMBLING BAGS
(Usually made out of green flannel)

Ace of diamonds
Ace of hearts
Agate *(darker shades)*
Alexandrite
Alfalfa
Allspice
Amazonite
Amber
Angel's turnip
Anise
Aventurine
Black cat bone
Bluebell
Brick dust
Buckeye
Burning bush
Calamus
Chalcedony
Chamomille
China berries
Chrysoprase
Coins

Damiana
Daffodil
Devil's shoestring
Dragon's blood reed
Dice (pair)
Dollar sign
Egyptian ankh
Four-leaf clover
Ginger root
Gold
Hazel
Heather
Heart of swallow
Holey stones
Holly
Jezebel root
Job's tears
Joe pie
Linden
Lepidolite
Little John chew
Lodestones (two)

Lucky hand
May apple
Mercury
Mustard seed
Myrtle
Nutmeg
Oak
Orange
Pearl
Persimmon
Pine
Pomegranate

Poppy
Rabbit's foot
Rose
Silver coin
Snakeroot
Star anise
Tiger's eye
Tonka beans
Turquoise
Vertivert
Violet

MONEY BAGS
(Red or green flannel)

Coins (silver)
Gold
Green candles

Image of St. Raymond
Lodestones (two)
Silver

PROTECTION BAGS
(Black leather or any other material)

African Violet
Agate (lighter shades)
Agrimony
Aloe vera
Alyssum
Amber
Angelica root
Anise
Apache tears

Arrowroot
Asafoetida
Azabache (jet stone)
Balm Gilead buds
Basil
Bay leaves
Birch
Black beans
Bladderwrack

Boneset
Bromeliad
Broom
Burdock
Cactus
Calamus
Camphor
Caraway
Carnelian
Carnation
Cedar
Chrysanthemum
Chain
Chalcedony
Chrysoprase
Cinnamon
Cinquefoil
Citrine
Clove
Clover
Coral
Crucifix
Cumin
Curry
Cyclamen
Cypress
Datura
Diamond
Dill
Dogwood
Dragon's blood
Elder
Elecampane
Eucalyptus
Emerald
Eye of bat

Fennel
Feverwort
Flax
Fleabane
Flint
Five finger grass
Foxglove
Frankincense
Galangal
Garlic
Garnet
Geranium
Ginseng
Graveyard Dirt
(blessed with holy water)
Heather
Heart of swallow
Holly
Holy water
Honeysuckle
Horehound
Houseleek
Hyacinth
Hyssop
Ivy
Jade
Jasper
John the Conqueror
Juniper
Lady's slipper
Lepidolite
Lapis
Larkspur
Lavender
Lilac
Lily

Linden
Lodestone with filings
Lotus
Lucky hand
Magnolia leaves
Malachite
Mallow
Mandrake
Marble
Marigold
Master of the woods
Mimosa
Mint
Mistletoe
Moonstone
Mother of pearl
Mugwort
Mulberry
Mullein
Mustard
Myrrh
Nettle
Oak
Obsidian
Olive oil
Olivine
Onion
Parsley
Patchouli
Pearl
Pennyroyal
Peony
Pepper
Periwinkle
Peridot
Petrified wood

Pine
Plantain
Prayer to the Just Judge
Prayer of St. Louis Bertrand
Primrose
Quartz crystal
Quince leaves
Radish
Rain water
Raspberry
Rattlesnake root
Red coral
Religious image of a saint
Rhubarb
River water
Rose
Rowan
Ruby
Rue
St. John's Wort
Sage
Salt
Saltpeter
Sandalwood
Sea horse
Silk cotton tree
Snapdragon
Southern John
Southernwood
Spanish moss
Staurolite
Sunstone
Sweet woodruff
Thistle
Tiger's eye
Topaz

Tourmaline, black
Trumpet weed
Tulip
Turquoise
Valerian
Vervain
Violet

Willow
Wintergreen
Witch hazel
Wolfbane
Wormwood
Wood betony
Yucca

OUANGA BAGS

As a general rule, Marie Laveau's ouanga bags are not meant to be kept, but sent to the persons we wish to harm, or buried in their vicinity. Practitioners tend to use either black or red flannel to make these hexing bags.

Army Ants
Asafoetida
Black candles
Black mustard seed
Black pepper
Cayenne pepper
Coffin
Dog grass
Dog shit
Goofer dust
Image of victim

Lime
Nails
Personal objects of victim
Pins
Scorpions
Snakes
Spiders
Tarantulas
Thorns
Tormentilla
Wasps

HEALTH BAGS
(black leather, white linen)

Agate, banded or green
Allspice
Amethyst
Apple
Aventurine
Azurite
Bamboo
Barley
Bay leaf
Betony
Blackberry
Blessed thistle
Bloodstone
Buckeye
Carnelian
Cedar
Chrysoprase
Cinnamon
Comfrey
Copper (coins or medal)
Coral
Diamond
Elder
Five Finger Grass

Flint
Garnet
Glass eye or marble
Hematite
High John the Conqueror
Holey stones
Jade
Jadejasper
Jet
Lapis lazuli
Laurel
Lemongrass
Life everlasting
Mustard seed
Peridot
Petrified wood
Quartz crystal
Saphire
Sodalite
Staurolite
Sugilite
Sunstone
Topaz
Turquoise

5

Prayers and Saints

SECRET NAMES OF THE SAINTS

The saints have names that only the gifted know, the two-headed people like us. The reason why we can summon the saints better and faster than normal folk is because we know the secret names of the saints.

St. Peter's secret name is LABA
St. Michael's is DANIEL BLANC
St. Anthony's YONSOO
St. Paul's ONZA TIER

INDISPENSABLE CATHOLIC PRAYERS

Let us not forget that besides being the undisputed queen of Voodoo in New Orleans, Marie Laveau was also a devout Catholic who had great faith in the powers of the Church. There were certain Catholic prayers that Marie recited daily, and some that she used as opening prayers in all of her Voodoo ceremonies. She considered *"The Apostle's Creed"* to be the most mystical of all Catholic prayers. It consists of twelve lines, each line made by a different apostle.

THE APOSTLE'S CREED

I believe in God the Father Almighty,
Maker of Heaven and Earth
And in Jesus Christ his only Son, Our Lord,
Who was conceived by the Holy Ghost,
born of the Virgin Mary;
Suffered under Pontius Pilate,
was crucified, dead, and buried;
He descended into hell;
On the third day he rose again from the dead.
He ascended into Heaven, and sitteth on the right
hand of God the Father Almighty.
From thence He shall come to judge
the quick and the dead.
I believe in the Holy Ghost;
In the Holy Catholic Church;
the communion of saints the forgiveness of sins
the resurrection of the body and life everlasting,
Amen.

FOR GAMBLING LUCK: Gamblers write this creed backwards, fold it around a Nutmeg, tie it with Green ribbon, anoint it with Fast Luck oil, and carry it with them as they gamble.

HAIL MARY

Hail Mary, full of grace
The Lord is with thee
Blessed art thou amongst women
And blessed is the fruit of thy womb, Jesus

Holy Mary, Mother of God
Pray for us sinners now,
and in the hour of our death, Amen.

PATER NOSTRUM

*(Our Father in Latin, thought to be more powerful and
the one in use in those far-gone days of pre-Vatican II
Christianity)*

Pater Nostrum qui es in caelis
Sanctificetur nomen tuum
Adveniat regnum tuum
Fait voluntas tua
Sictus caelo et in terra
Panem nostrum cotidanum
Da nobis hodie
Ot dimitte nobis debita
Nostra sicut et nos dimittimus
Debitoribus nostris
Et ne nos inducas in tentationem
Set libera nos a malo.
Amen

OUR FATHER

Our Father who art in heaven
Hollowed be Thy name
Thy kingdom come
Thy wilt be done
On earth as it is in heaven
Give us each day our daily bread
and forgive us our debts
as we forgive our debtors
and lead us not into temptation
but deliver us from evil
Amen

THE MAGNIFICAT

This prayer, taken from the Bible, is thought by Voodoos and other magicians to be one of the most potent of all. Carry it with you for protection from all evil.

My soul doth magnify the Lord
And my spirit has rejoiced in God my savior
For he hath regarded the low state of his handmaiden:
For, behold, from henceforth all generations
shall call me blessed.
For he that is mighty hath done to me great things;
And holy is his name.
And his mercy is on them that fear him.
From generation to generation
He hath shewed strength with his arm;
He hath scattered the proud in the imagination of their hearts.
He hath put down the mighty from their seats,
And exalted them of low degree.
He hath filled the hungry with good things;
And the rich he hath sent empty away.
He hath holpen his servant Israel,
In rememberance of his mercy;
As he spake to our fathers,
To Abraham and to his seed for ever.

GLORIA

Glory be to the Father,
Glory be to the Son,
and Glory be to the Holy Ghost.
As it was in the beginning,
now and always and forever and ever,
world without end
Amen.

THE 23RD PSALM

The Lord is my shepherd; I shall not want
He maketh me to lie down in green pastures:
He leadeth me beside the still waters.
He restoreth my soul
He leadeth me in the paths of righteousness
For his name's sake.
Yea, though I walk through the
valley of the shadow of death,
I will fear no evil: for thou art with me:
Thy rod and thy staff they comfort me.
Thou preparest a table before me
In the presence of mine enemies:
Thou anointest my head with oil:
My cup runneth over.
Surely goodness and mercy shall follow me
All the days of my life
And I will dwell in the house of the Lord for ever.

PRAYER TO MARIE LAVEAU

Eh Yé Yé Mamzelle,
Ya, yé, yé, li konin tou, gris-gris
Li, ti, kowri, avec vieux kikordi;
Oh ouai, yé Mamzelle Marie
Le konin bien li Grand Zombi!
Kan sóléid te kashe,
li té sorti Bayou,
Pou, apprened le Voudou,
Oh, tingouar, yé hén hén,
Oh tingouar, yé éh éh,
Li appé vini, li Grand Zombi,
Li appé vini, pol fé mouri!

OPENING PRAYER
FOR VOODOO CEREMONIES

Marie Laveau taught her English-speaking disciples the following opening song:

St. Peter, St. Peter, open the door. Come, Papa Lemba, I'm calling you, Come to me! St. Peter, St. Peter, open the door.

HE-RON MANDE

Marie Laveau sang this hymn before petitioning her spirits. Do the best you can with the pronunciation, the spirits will appreciate your effort.

He-ron mandé
He-ron mandé,
Tigui li papa,
He-ron mandé,
Tigui li papa,
He-ron mandé,
He-ron mandé,
He-ron mandé,
Do se dan do-go.

SAINTS AND DEITIES
YOU SHOULD PETITION
TO OPEN DOORS
(Red and black, or orange candle)

Baron Cimitiere	Lucero
Eleggua	Mercury
Loki	St. Peter

Papa Legma, Limbo, Lamba

FOR LOVE
(use pink or red candle)

Aphrodite	Erzulie Freda Dahomey
Cupid	Anima Sola (Lonely Soul)
Cybele	Mamam Bregitte
Hathor	Our Lady of Charity
Ishtar	St. Anthony
Isis	Shango
Kama	Venus
Oshun	Mary Magdalene

TO INCREASE BUSINESS
(Use green candle)

Athena	Eleggua
Ebisu	Oya
Jupiter	St. Joseph
Midas	

TO INCREASE BRAIN POWER
(Use white candle)

Artemis
Damballah
Saraswati
Obatala

TO EXPEDITE MATTERS
(Use white or yellow candle)

St. Expedito

TRIUMPH OVER ENEMIES
(White candle)

Ogun   St. Michael
St. Barbara   Shango
St. George

TO GET A JOB
(Blue candle)

St. Joseph

HEALTH
(White or blue candle)

Virgin Mary   St. Lazarus
Aesculapius   *(blood diseases, contagion)*
Raphael   St. Lucy *(eyes)*
Inle

FINANCIAL SUCCESS
(Green or gold candle)

Lakshmi   Olokun
Oshun   St. Peter

VISITING THE TOMB OF
THE SAINTED MARIE

In New Orleans, thousands go to St. Louis Cemetery, where Marie Laveau is entombed in an above-ground crypt. Tradition has it that if you approach her tomb with respect, draw three x's on the side of her crypt using red brick, and offer her a libation of water and a silver dollar, Mam'zelle, as her devotees call her, will grant your wish. Old Willie Glapion, my Voodoo teacher, was taciturn and gruff, but a wiser and gentler soul I've yet to meet. He advised me not to do the cemetery ritual as popularly performed.

"My Grandmama would not approve of this leave a dollar, paint three crosses bullshit." Smiling a rare smile, the old man proceeded to say: "Marie Laveau was too high-up to do anything for a dollar!"

Willie told me the best way to petition his grandmother was to ask for money, a particular amount, and promise a particular percentage once the money came through.

"Write the amount using pigeon's blood on parchment, take it to her grave, go around it three times, kiss the floor, and leave"

"And how do I give your grandmother the money, since she is dead?" I asked my Voodoo teacher.

"Well, you can give it to me" Willie noticed I wasn't biting on that one. " Or you can donate it to the orphanage run by St. Louis Cathedral, Marie really did love that church."

VOODOO
& HOODOO

JIM HASKINS

$12.95

VOODOO & HOODOO
by Jim Haskins

Their Traditional Crafts
Revealed by Actual Practitioners

VOODOO MEN, HOODOO WOMEN & ROOT
DOCTORS... say they know how to use eggs,
graveyard dust; forks in the road; the numbers
3,7,and 9; pins and nails; red flannel bags; yellow
homespun; urine,feces, and blood; shoes and
clothing; black cats and black hens; doorsteps; and
the interior and exterior corners of houses to
conjure good and to conjure evil. Voodoo & Hoodoo
tells how these spiritual descendents of African
medicine men and sorcerers "lay tricks" and work
their magic, and explains the hold these practices
have had on their believers, from the Old World
origins until today.

ORIGINAL PUBLICATIONS · TOLL FREE 1 (888) OCCULT-1

$8.95

VOODOO
CHARMS & TALISMANS
by Robert Pelton

The Power of Voodoo can be yours today!
Absolutely authentic and easy to follow instructions to:

- Make your own talismans
- Concoct your own Love Potions
- Win at games of Chance
- Summon Spirits
- Defend yourself against those
  who may wish you ill
- Attack your enemies through
  devastating spells

Here are the words, the symbols and the ingredients.
Here is all you need to know to possess power.
beyond your imagination!

ORIGINAL PUBLICATIONS • TOLL FREE 1 (888) OCCULT-1